Garden Fairies Letter Writing

Published by Top That! Publishing plc
Tide Mill Way, Woodbridge, Suffolk, IP12 1AP
www.topthatpublishing.com

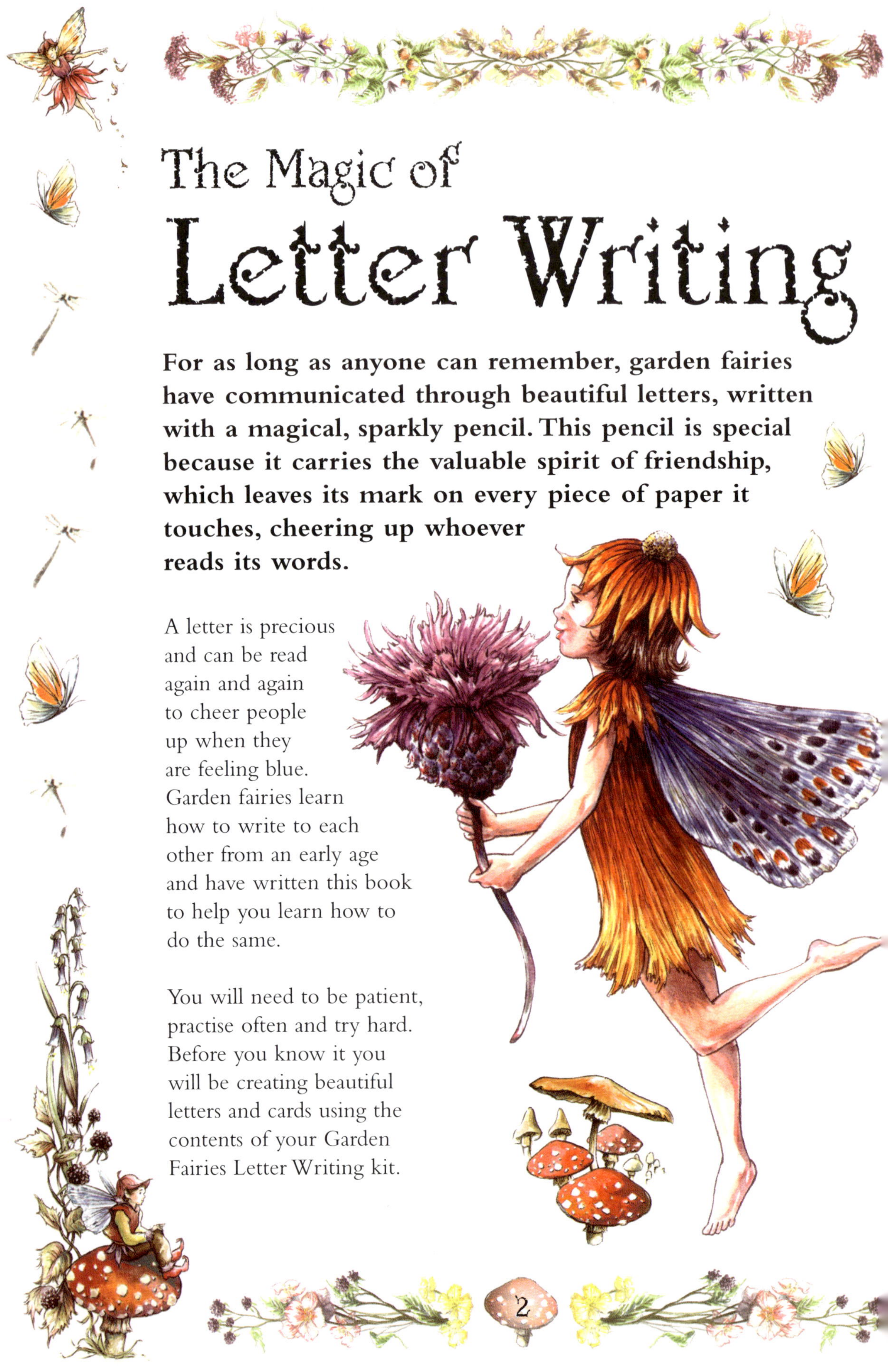

The Magic of Letter Writing

For as long as anyone can remember, garden fairies have communicated through beautiful letters, written with a magical, sparkly pencil. This pencil is special because it carries the valuable spirit of friendship, which leaves its mark on every piece of paper it touches, cheering up whoever reads its words.

A letter is precious and can be read again and again to cheer people up when they are feeling blue. Garden fairies learn how to write to each other from an early age and have written this book to help you learn how to do the same.

You will need to be patient, practise often and try hard. Before you know it you will be creating beautiful letters and cards using the contents of your Garden Fairies Letter Writing kit.

The Alphabet

When we write words, we take letters of the alphabet and put them into the order we need to make words. Some letters are used more often than others. The letter e is used more than any other letter in the alphabet.

Take a look at the alphabet below.

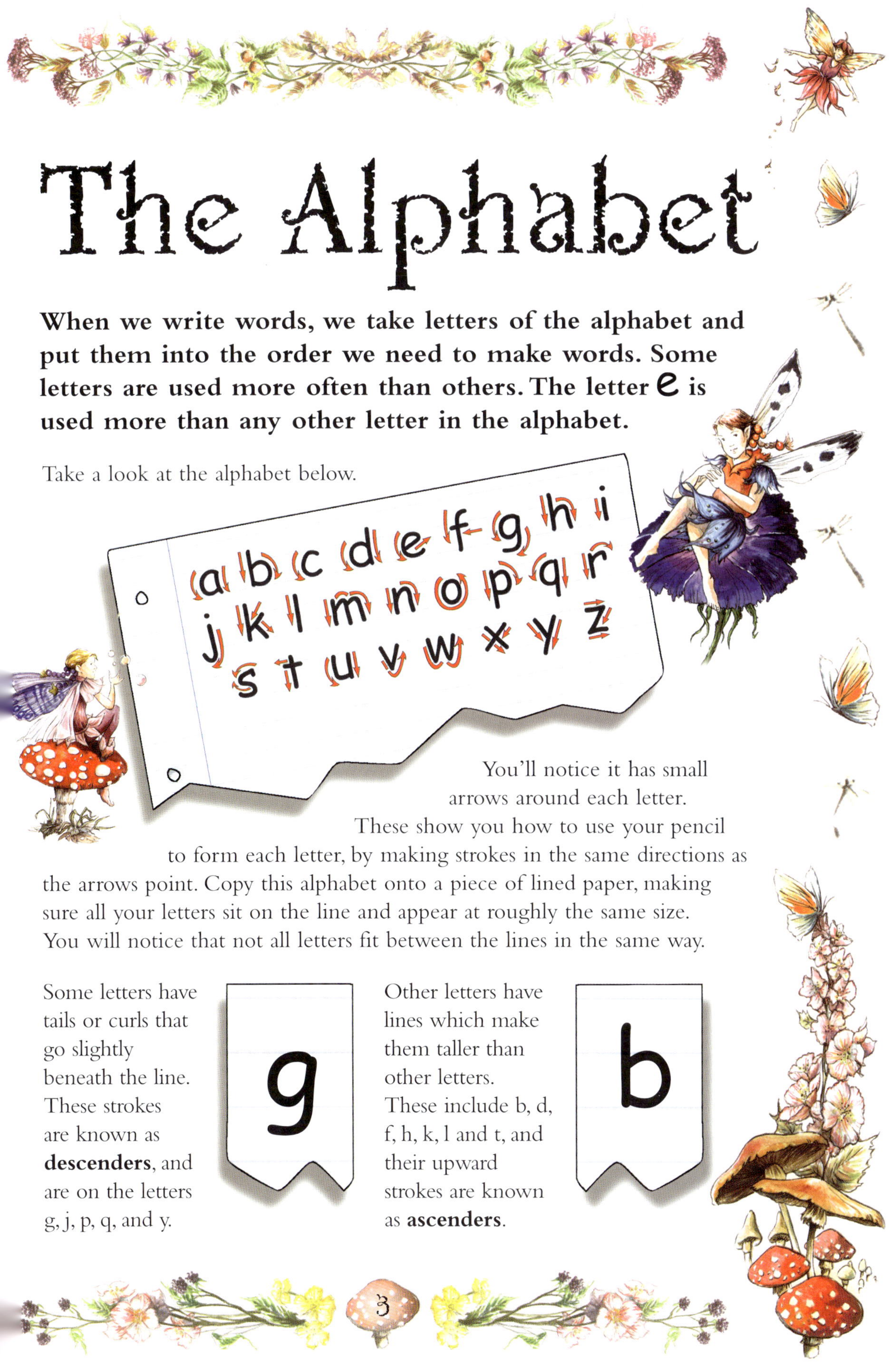

You'll notice it has small arrows around each letter. These show you how to use your pencil to form each letter, by making strokes in the same directions as the arrows point. Copy this alphabet onto a piece of lined paper, making sure all your letters sit on the line and appear at roughly the same size. You will notice that not all letters fit between the lines in the same way.

Some letters have tails or curls that go slightly beneath the line. These strokes are known as **descenders**, and are on the letters g, j, p, q, and y.

Other letters have lines which make them taller than other letters. These include b, d, f, h, k, l and t, and their upward strokes are known as **ascenders**.

Capital letters

Capital letters are also known as **upper case** letters or **big** letters.

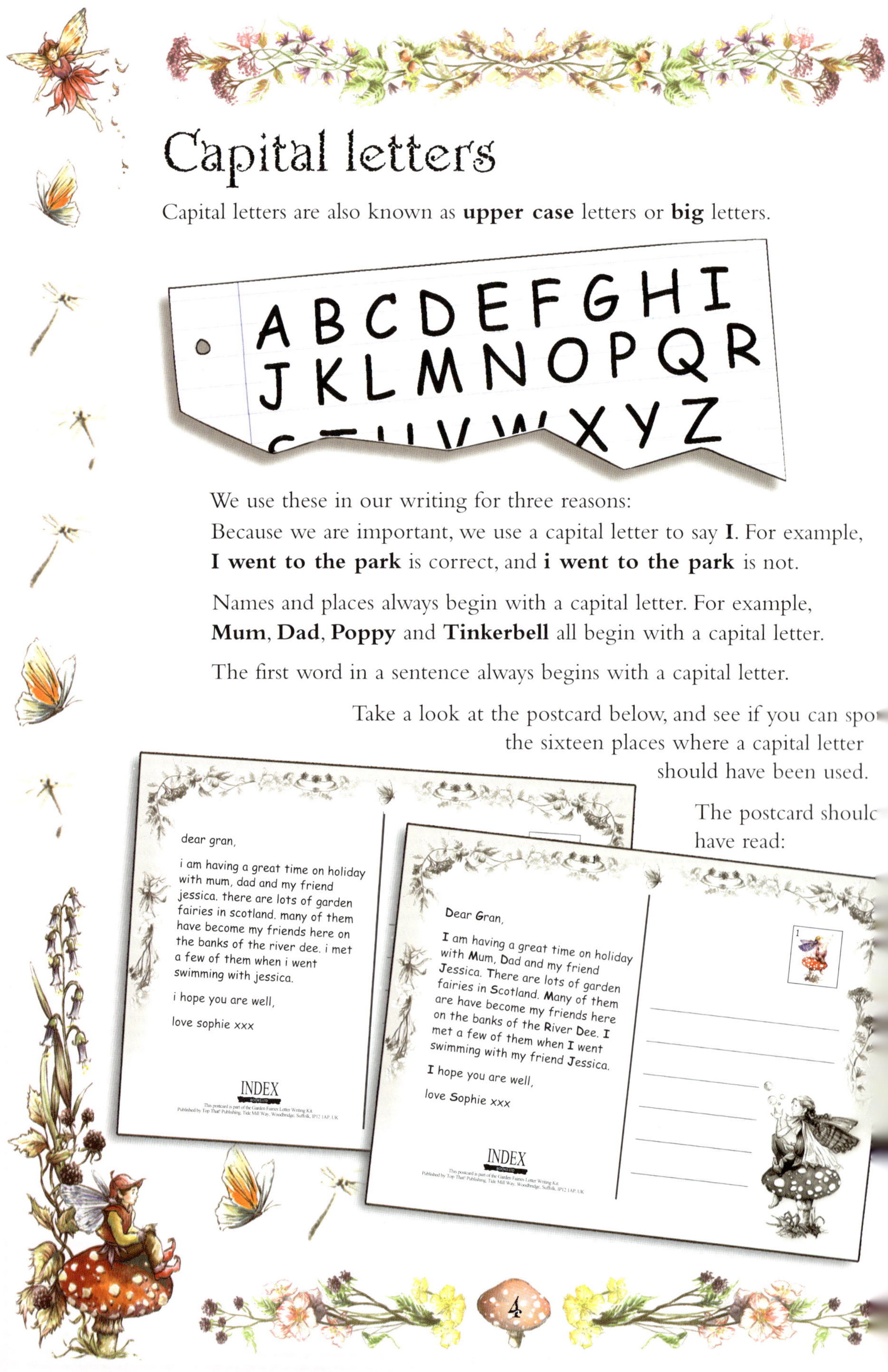

We use these in our writing for three reasons:

Because we are important, we use a capital letter to say **I**. For example, **I went to the park** is correct, and **i went to the park** is not.

Names and places always begin with a capital letter. For example, **Mum**, **Dad**, **Poppy** and **Tinkerbell** all begin with a capital letter.

The first word in a sentence always begins with a capital letter.

Take a look at the postcard below, and see if you can spo the sixteen places where a capital letter should have been used.

The postcard shoulc have read:

Perfect Punctuation

Punctuation means putting marks and spaces into your sentences so that people can understand them more easily. You'll find, listed below, a few examples of punctuation, and how best to use them to improve your sentences.

Full stops

Full stops are little dots that come at the end of a sentence to show it has finished. When we see one of these, we know we can stop to take a breath. Look at the text below. Each full stop is shown in bold to show you where they go.

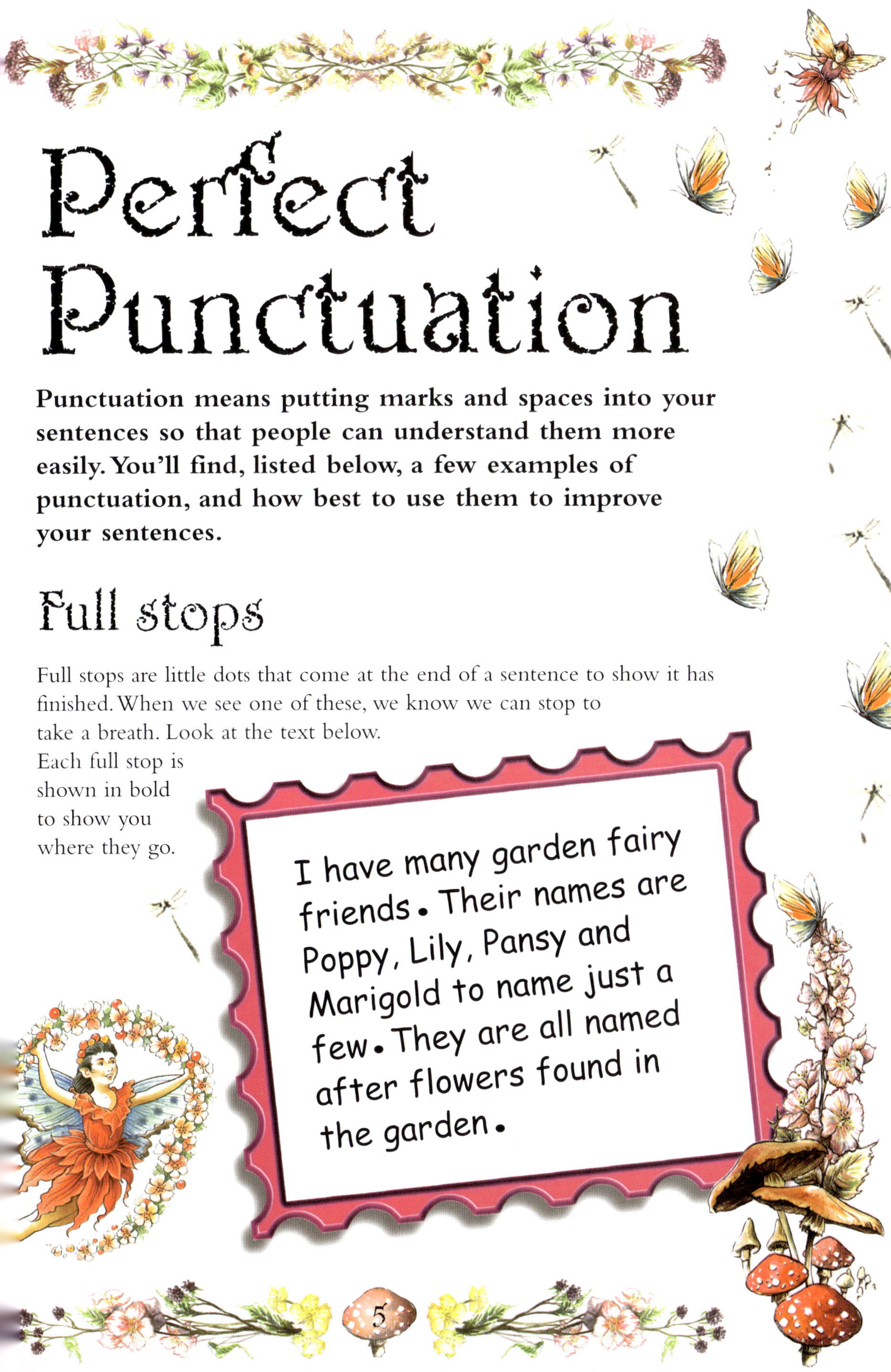

Commas

A comma tells us we should pause for breath in a sentence, but not stop altogether because the sentence isn't over. Commas are used to make the text flow more smoothly. Look at the text opposite to see an example of how this works.

A garden fairy is faster than the blink of an eye, as light as a feather, and extremely shy.

Brackets

Brackets are also useful things to use in your writing. They have the effect of making sections of your writing sound whispered, or provide extra detail to break up the body of your writing and stop it from being too long. Look at the example opposite to see how this can be used.

The garden fairy jumped down from the toadstool and twitched her wings in the evening breeze. She tried to look away (not wanting to seem too interested) but couldn't help pricking her ears up to hear what the elves were whispering.

Paragraphs

A paragraph is a group of sentences that are all about the same subject. You begin a new paragraph by leaving a gap between the blocks of text you have written.

Look at the Thank You letter below. It is divided into two paragraphs, each talking about a different thing.

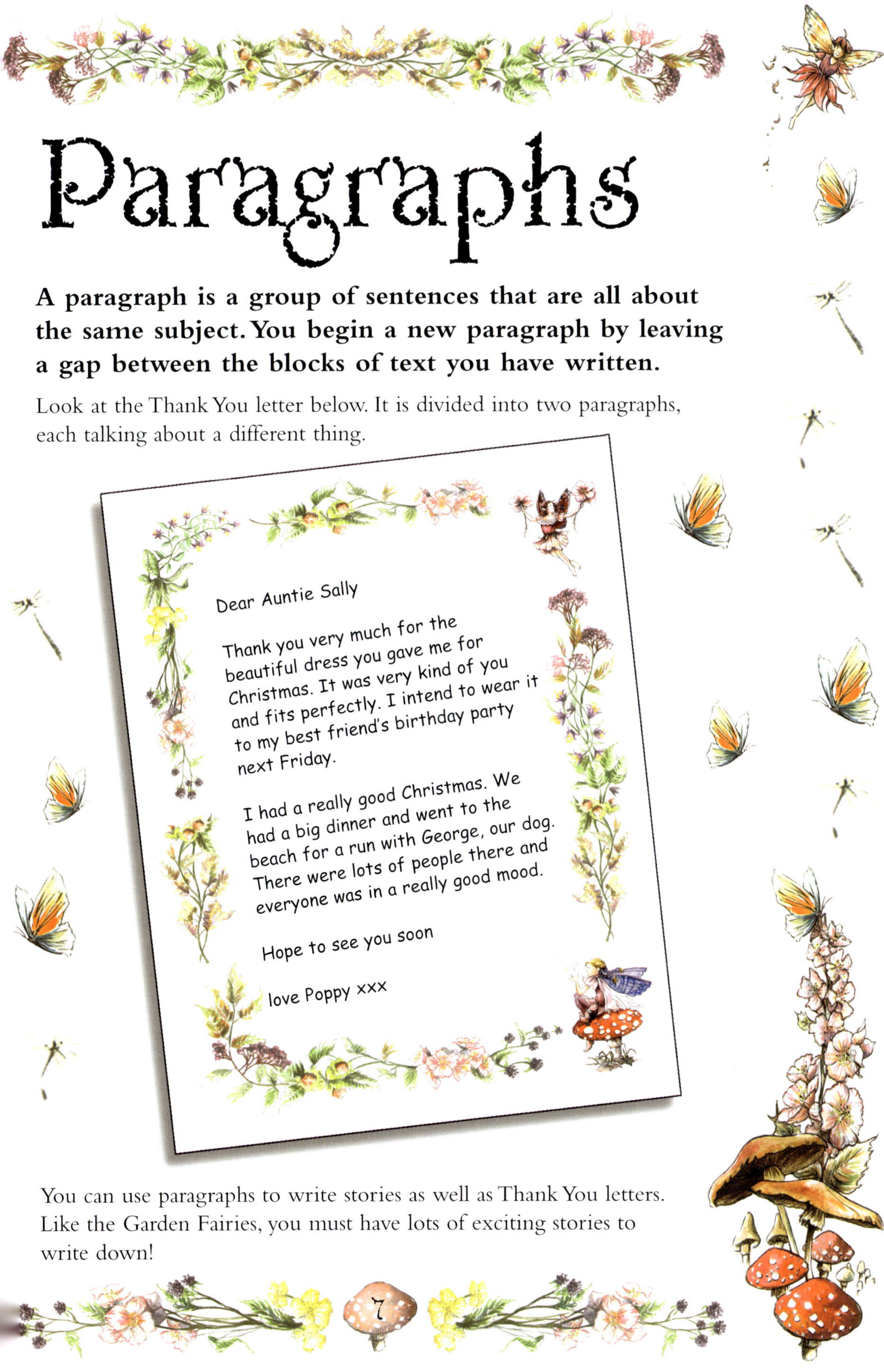

Dear Auntie Sally

Thank you very much for the beautiful dress you gave me for Christmas. It was very kind of you and fits perfectly. I intend to wear it to my best friend's birthday party next Friday.

I had a really good Christmas. We had a big dinner and went to the beach for a run with George, our dog. There were lots of people there and everyone was in a really good mood.

Hope to see you soon

love Poppy xxx

You can use paragraphs to write stories as well as Thank You letters. Like the Garden Fairies, you must have lots of exciting stories to write down!

Simple Spelling

The next step in writing beautiful letters is making sure your words are spelled correctly. Many words are spelled how they sound, but unless you are sure of a spelling, it is best to look it up in a dictionary. This is very easy to do.

To look something up in a dictionary, you need to know what letter it starts with. Let's start by looking up the word **toadstool**.

It starts with a **t**.

Sound the word out to find out the second letter.

It is **o**.

Turn to the page with all the words beginning with **to**.

The **to** letters come after those beginning with **ta**, **te**, **th** and **ti**.

It should be amongst the first of the **to** words, because the next letter in toadstool is **a**.

If you practise using your dictionary often, before you know it you'll be able to look words up in no time. After a while, you will be able to spell so well, you won't need to use a dictionary very often at all.

Would **Fairy** come before **Flying** in the dictionary? And would **Wonderful** come before **Wings**?

After a while, you will be able to spell so well, you won't need to use a dictionary very often at all.

Taking Messages

If you want to write a note to tell someone you called round and they weren't in, or that someone 'phoned for them and you have taken a message, all you need to write on your paper is the time, who the message is from and any other important information.

4 pm

Hi Poppy,

Just called round to see if you would like to come to my tea party tomorrow afternoon. Give me a call by 6 pm or just come round.

See you later,

Tinkerbell xxx

pm is a short way to say afternoon or evening.

am means morning.

You also might have to write down some messages you take when someone telephones. Just as for the message opposite, begin by writing down the time of the call, before picking out the important bits of the message and writing these down. The text below is an example of a telephone call. Underneath it is the message Fairy Forget-me-not took for her friend.

"Hello, Forget-me-not. This is Primrose calling for Fairy Lavender, is she there? Oh, dear – well, would you mind asking her to ring me about the fittings for the bridesmaid dresses for Fairy Buttercup's wedding? I have made an appointment for next Tuesday, and wanted to make sure she could make it or I will cancel. Can she please let me know by tomorrow afternoon? Thank you so much. She has my number..."

2 pm

Lavender,

Primrose called. She wants to know if you can make it to a dress fitting appointment, for Buttercup's wedding, on Tuesday. Please call her back tonight or tomorrow morning.

Forget-me-not

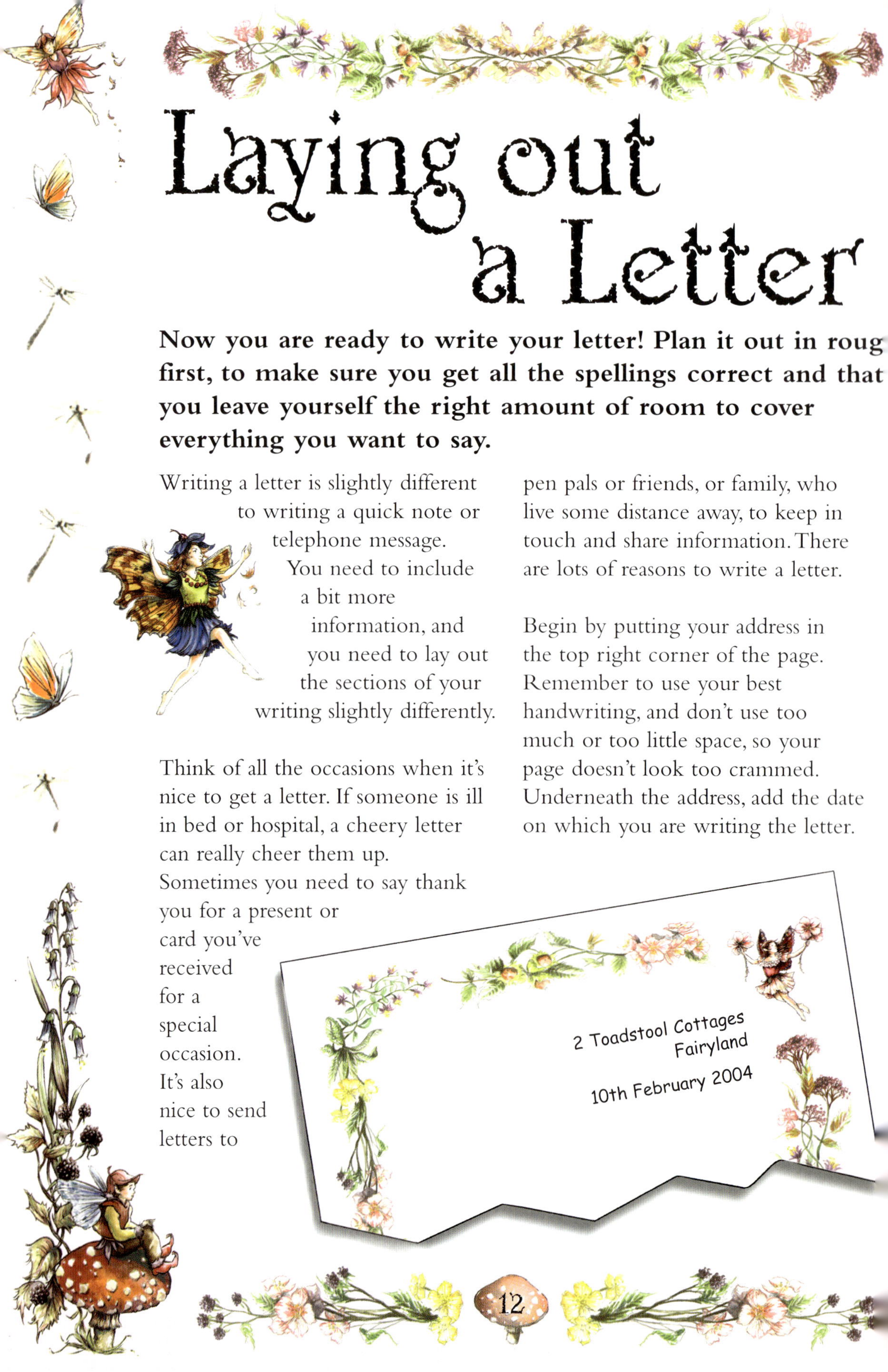

Laying out a Letter

Now you are ready to write your letter! Plan it out in roug first, to make sure you get all the spellings correct and that you leave yourself the right amount of room to cover everything you want to say.

Writing a letter is slightly different to writing a quick note or telephone message. You need to include a bit more information, and you need to lay out the sections of your writing slightly differently.

Think of all the occasions when it's nice to get a letter. If someone is ill in bed or hospital, a cheery letter can really cheer them up. Sometimes you need to say thank you for a present or card you've received for a special occasion. It's also nice to send letters to pen pals or friends, or family, who live some distance away, to keep in touch and share information. There are lots of reasons to write a letter.

Begin by putting your address in the top right corner of the page. Remember to use your best handwriting, and don't use too much or too little space, so your page doesn't look too crammed. Underneath the address, add the date on which you are writing the letter.

Now write Dear – to the left of the page, underneath the area filled by the address on the right. You are ready to start your letter slightly below this.

More formal letters, such as the kind business people write, also have the address of the person you are writing to in the top left corner. That makes your page look like this...

Page planning

Remember to plan your page properly before you begin. Write out all the text you want to include in rough first, so you will know how much space you have to fit your words into and make it look as nice as possible. This way, when you write up your letter for real, it will fit on the page well and look really special.

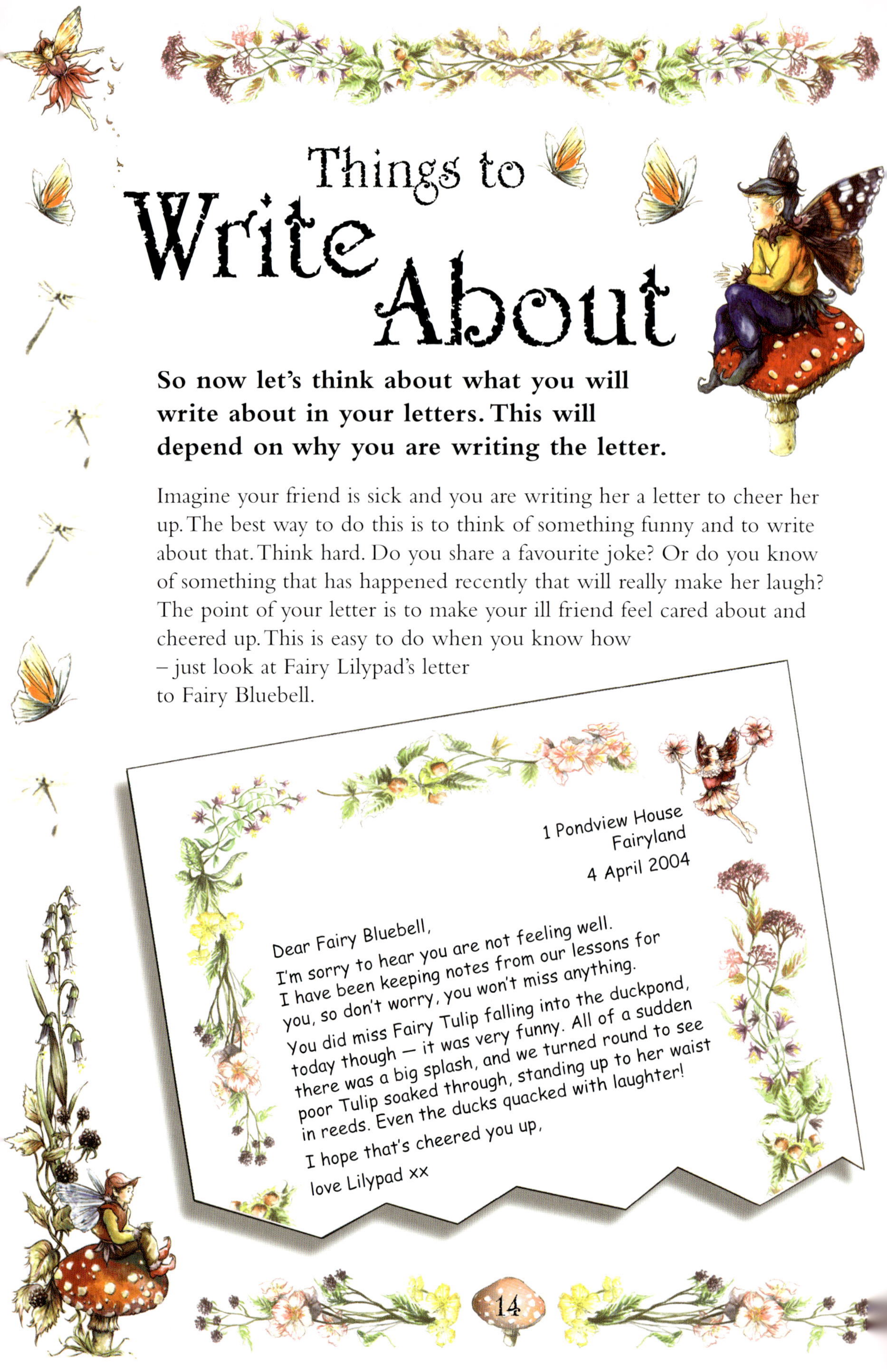

Things to Write About

So now let's think about what you will write about in your letters. This will depend on why you are writing the letter.

Imagine your friend is sick and you are writing her a letter to cheer her up. The best way to do this is to think of something funny and to write about that. Think hard. Do you share a favourite joke? Or do you know of something that has happened recently that will really make her laugh? The point of your letter is to make your ill friend feel cared about and cheered up. This is easy to do when you know how – just look at Fairy Lilypad's letter to Fairy Bluebell.

1 Pondview House
Fairyland
4 April 2004

Dear Fairy Bluebell,

I'm sorry to hear you are not feeling well. I have been keeping notes from our lessons for you, so don't worry, you won't miss anything.

You did miss Fairy Tulip falling into the duckpond, today though – it was very funny. All of a sudden there was a big splash, and we turned round to see poor Tulip soaked through, standing up to her waist in reeds. Even the ducks quacked with laughter!

I hope that's cheered you up,

love Lilypad xx

Look at the ideas below to help you decide what to write about if you're stuck for ideas.

Thank you letters

Write about how and when you will use the present you have been given, and how you enjoyed the event they gave you a present for.

Dear Auntie Sarah,

Thank you so much for the painting set you sent me for my birthday. It was really kind and I have already had a lot of fun using it to do portraits of my friends.

I had a really great birthday. I went ice skating with my friends and then we had a pizza and watched a video.

See you soon,

love Fairy Daffodil xx

Pen pal letters

You won't have seen a pen pal for a long time, if at all, so it's a good idea to write about the things you have been doing since you last got in touch. Try to remember any interesting places you have visited, films you have seen, books you have read or any praise or prizes you have won through school, sports or musical activities. These subjects are also good for when you are writing to relatives you have not seen in a while.

Addressing your Envelope

It is very important to address your envelope clearly and correctly because if it is hard to read or wrongly addressed, your prized letter might never get to the person you have written to!

Start writing the name and address about halfway down the envelope, so that there is enough room at the top right corner for the stamp and the marks of the post office.

Informal

This is how to write an envelope:

Formal

Another way to write an envelope is like this:

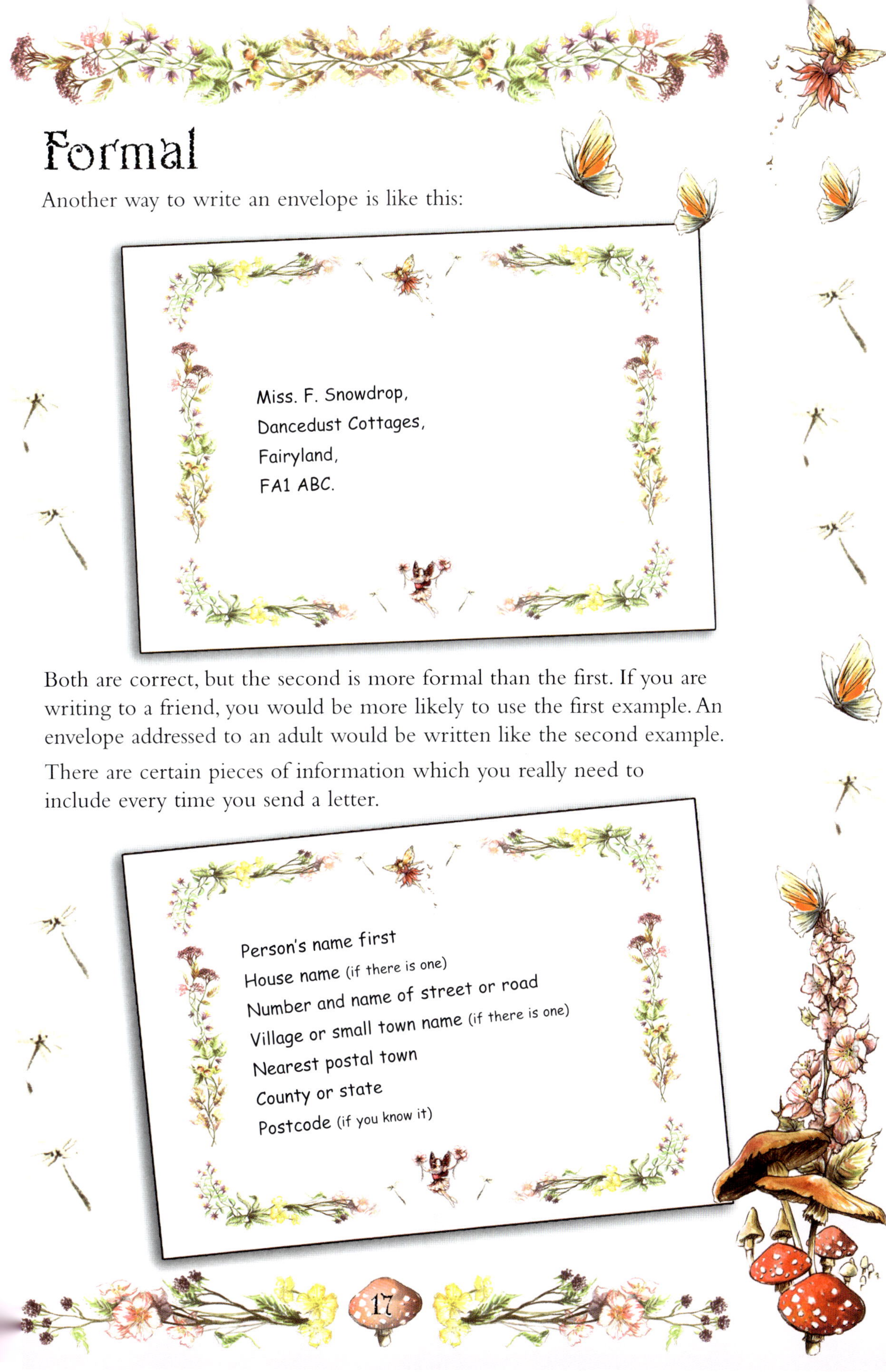

Both are correct, but the second is more formal than the first. If you are writing to a friend, you would be more likely to use the first example. An envelope addressed to an adult would be written like the second example.

There are certain pieces of information which you really need to include every time you send a letter.

Letter Games

Test your letter writing skills with these fun games!

Missing link

Can you tell which letters are missing from these words?

Scrambled paragraphs

The paragraphs in Fairy Foxglove's note to Fairy Rosebud have become a little scrambled. Can you tell from what she is saying which order the paragraphs should go in? *(answers at foot of page)*

Dear Fairy Rosebud,

(C) We had seafood in river reeds; it tasted very nice and exotic. I also drank lots of elderflower water as it was very hot.

(A) Just a quick note to tell you about my holiday. I decided to fly myself rather than take a plane, and landed just in time for dinner.

(M) I'll have to bring them around to show you sometime!

(P) The next day I went to the top of a mountain and got some really brilliant photographs of the view.

(T) Then I went to sunbathe and do some watersports. It was very different to splashing around in the pond, and I soon worked off my big dinner!

love

Fairy Foxglove xxx

Answers: 1(A) 2(C) 3(T) 4(P) 5(M)

Fairy Friends

Keep a record of your friends' and family's addresses and birthdays, so their details are never far away when you want to write a letter to them.

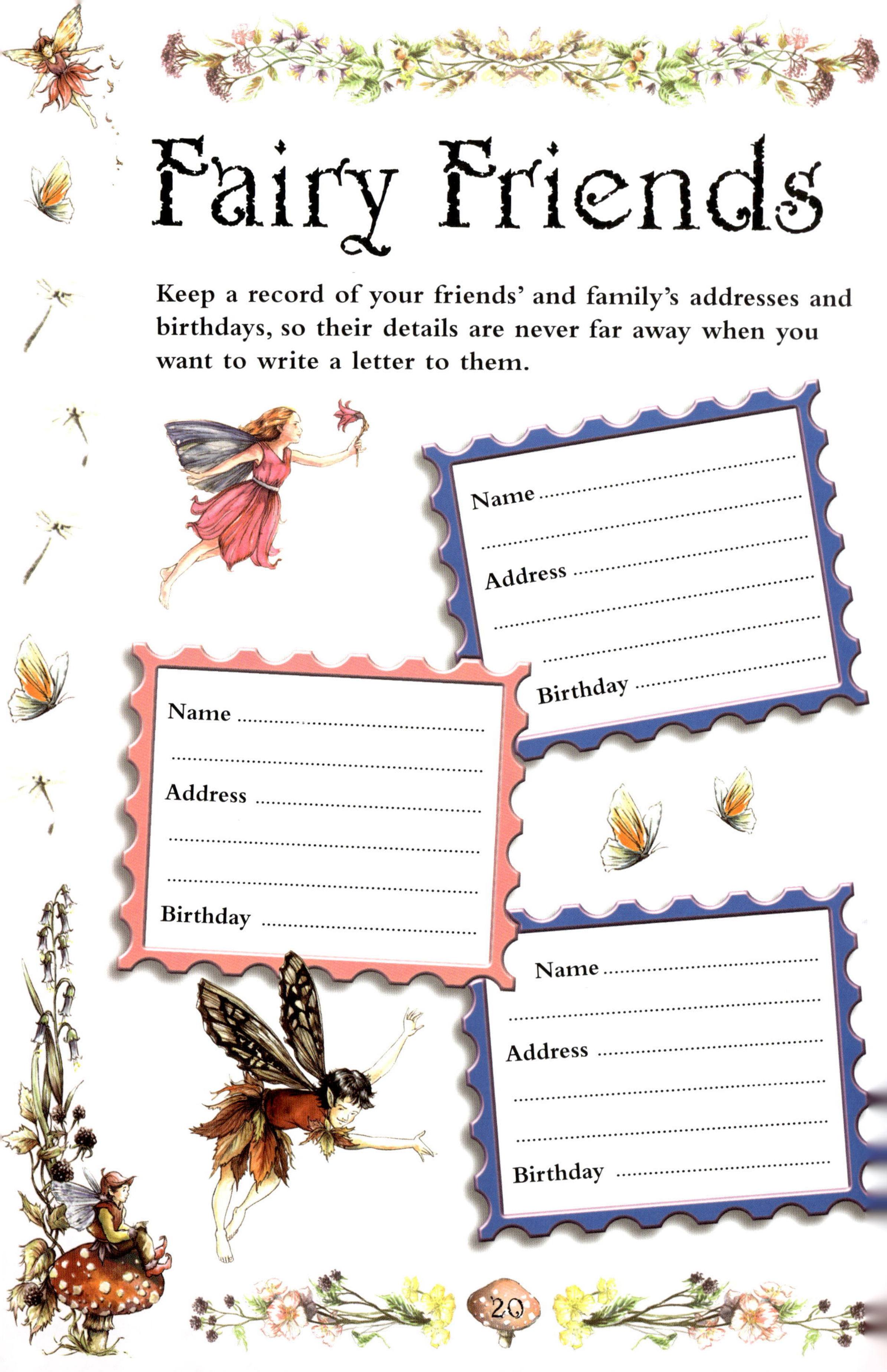

Name ....

....

Address ....

....

....

Birthday ....

Name ....

....

Address ....

....

....

Birthday ....

Name ....

....

Address ....

....

....

Birthday ....

Name ....

....

Address ....

....

....

Birthday ....

Name ....

....

Address ....

....

....

Birthday ....

Name ....

....

Address ....

....

....

Birthday ....

Name ....

....

Address ....

....

....

Birthday ....

Name
Address
Birthday
Name
Address
Birthday
Name
Address
Birthday
Name
Address
Birthday

Name
Address
Birthday
Name
Address
Birthday
Name
Address
Birthday
Name
Address
Birthday

Name ....
....
Address ....
....
....
Birthday ....

Name ....
....
Address ....
....
....
Birthday ....

Name ....
....
Address ....
....
....
Birthday ....

Name ....
....
Address ....
....
....
Birthday ....